SKILLS ALL LAWYERS WISH THEY KNEW – MICROSOFT WORD EDITION

Haiqa Baig

Copyright

© Haiqa Baig, 2023

All rights reserved. No part of this guide may be reproduced, stored in a retrieval system, or transmitted, in any form or by any means, electronic, mechanical, photocopying, recording or otherwise, without prior permission of the copyright owner.

Disclaimer

This guide is for information only. While every effort has been made to check the accuracy and quality of the information given in this guide, neither the author nor the publisher accept any responsibility for the subsequent use of this information, for any errors or omissions that it may contain, or for any misunderstandings arising from it.

Any images visible in the "Example" or "How to Use" sections have been used for educational purposes only and created from Microsoft Office Word 2021.

Table of Contents

1. Track Changes 3
2. Using Comments 6
3. Replace Words Easily Throughout A Document 10
4. Finding Key Words and Phrases 13
5. Changing "Cases" Without Re-Typing The Whole Paragraph 15
6. Delete Extra Pages 17
7. Insert Page Numbers 19
8. Add Execution/Signature Pages 22
9. Comparing Documents 27
10. Combining Documents 31
11. Using Watermarks 35
12. Inserting Rows In Tables Faster 38
13. Copy and Paste Text Without Re-Formatting 40
14. Formatting Contents Page 43
15. Inserting Clause Numbers 46
16. Cross Reference and Hyperlink Clause Numbers 48
17. Protect The Document 52
18. Convert The Document To A PDF (Portable Document Format) 54

1. Track Changes

Benefits

- Makes it easier to see what amendments have been made to a document, by whom and when they were made;
- You can accept or reject the suggested amendments; and
- Beneficial to use when you are battling time constraints/ deadlines for documents to be agreed and served on respective parties.

Example

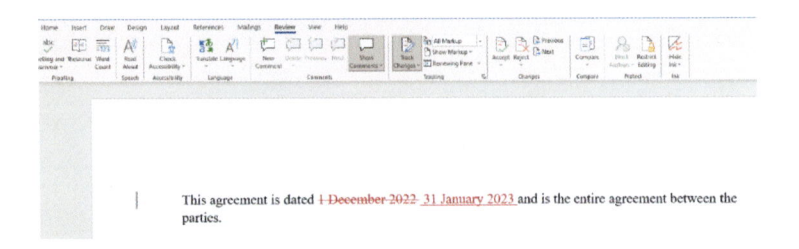

How to use

1. Click on the "*Review*" tab:

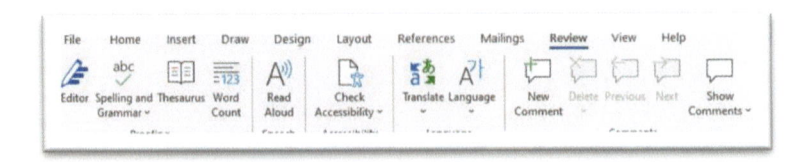

2. Click on "*Track Changes*" and start amending the document:

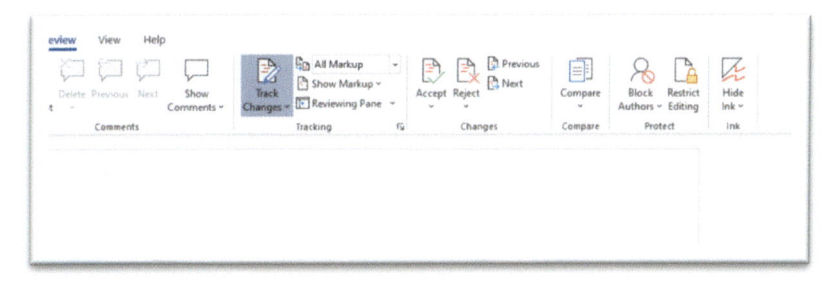

3. If you would like to:
    a. See who made the changes and when, you need to hover your mouse over those changes.
    b. Accept or reject specific changes, you can click "*accept this change*" or "*reject this change*" and move to next/previous change:

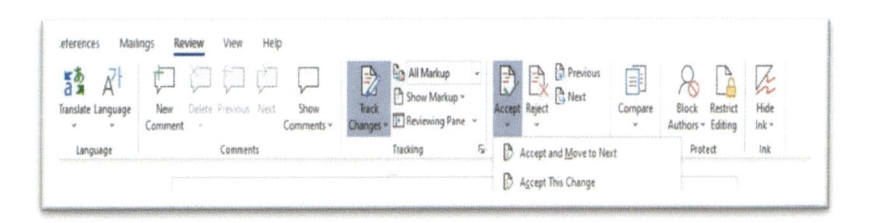

c. Accept or reject all changes, you can click *"accept all changes"* or *"reject all changes"*:

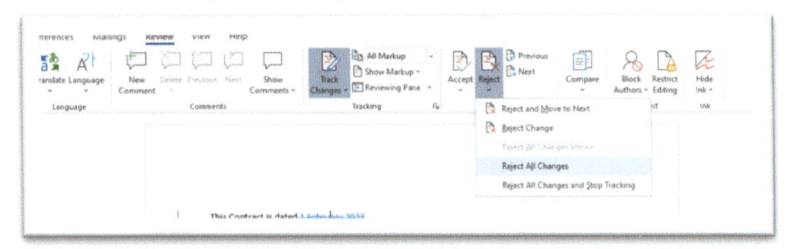

d. Hide the changes if they are being shown or show the changes if they are currently hidden, you can click on the line in the margin on either side of the document:

4. Click on *"Track Changes"* to turn off further amendments.

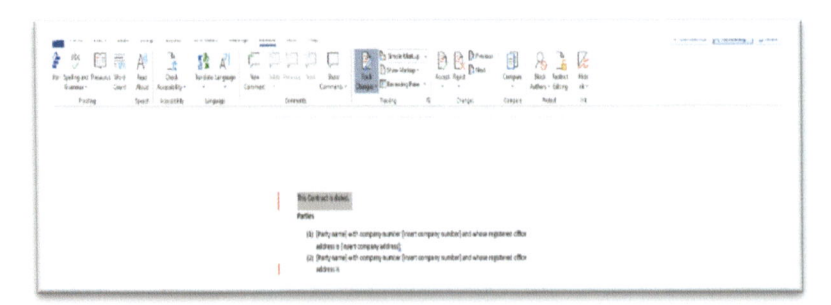

2. Using Comments

Benefits

- More efficient for parties to acknowledge and respond to specific points raised, which is highly beneficial for clients, experts, supervising junior lawyers and negotiating documents with other lawyers;
- Shows who made the comment and when; and
- Allows multiple parties to share their opinion.

Example

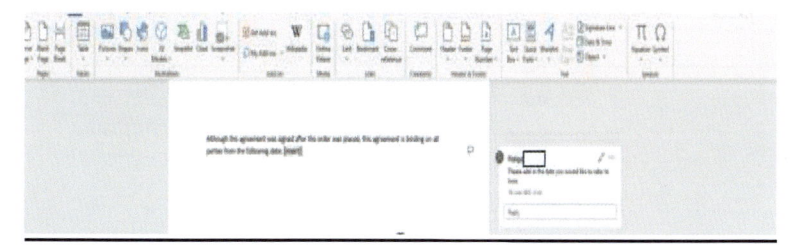

How to use

1. Select on the sentence/ text you intend on commenting on:

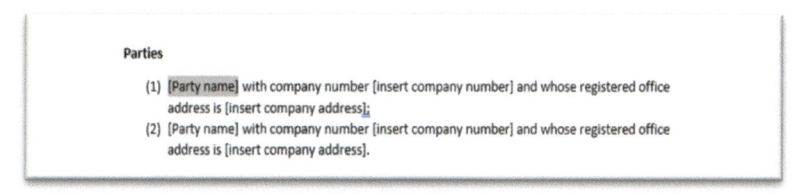

2. Click on the "*Review*" tab:

3. Click on "*New comment*" and insert your comment inside the box on the side of the document's margin:

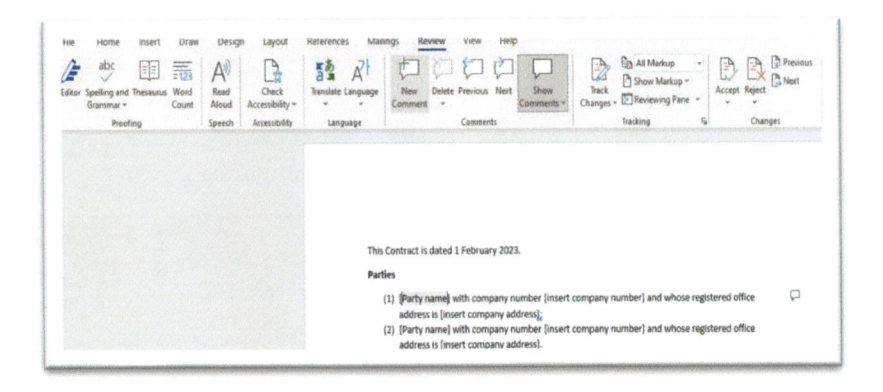

4. If you would like to:
   a. Reply to a comment, you can click on the "*Reply*" button in the comment and insert your response:

   b. Delete a specific comment, you can right click on the comment and select "*Delete*":

   c. Delete all comments, you can click "*Delete*" in the "*Review*" tab and subsequently click "*Delete All Comments in Document*":

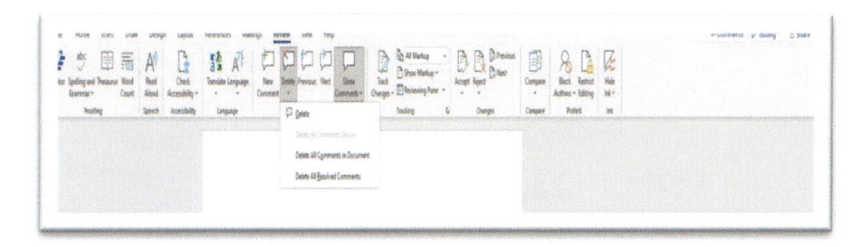

d. Show the comment has been dealt with and no further action is required, click "*Resolve*" on the relevant comment:

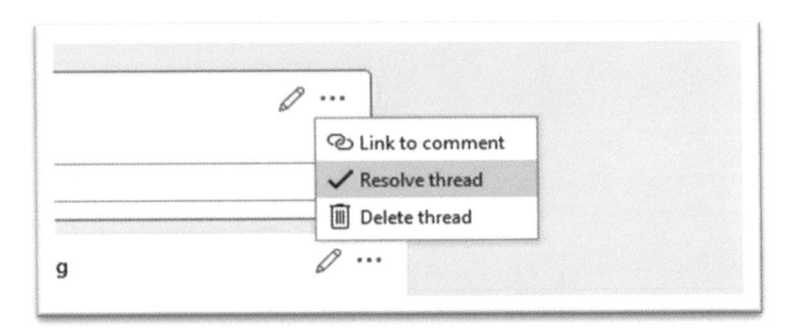

3. Replace Words Easily Throughout A Document

Benefits

- Less time consuming, as it changes all those specific words/phrases as you have requested;
- Allows you to focus on the content of the document; and
- Prevents you from forgetting to replace each and every word/phrase.

Example

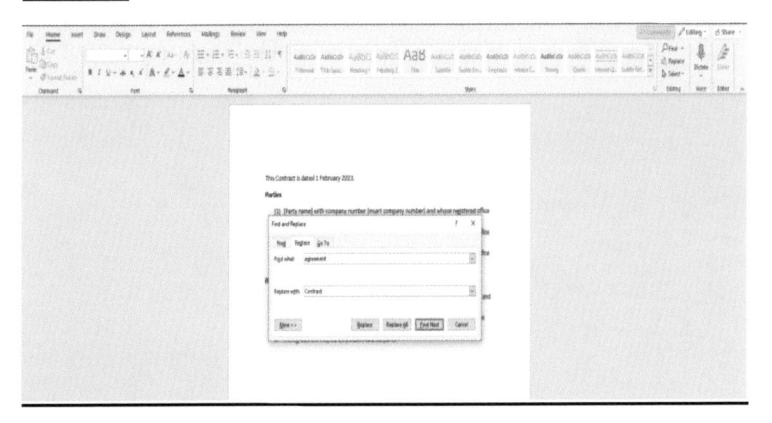

How to use

1. Click on the "*Home*" tab.
2. Click on "*Replace*":

3. In the "*find what*" or "*search for*" box, insert the word/ phrase you intend on replacing:

Find and Replace	? ×
Fin**d** Re**p**lace **G**o To	
Fi**n**d what: contract	⌄

4. In the "*Replace with*" box, insert the word/phrase you would like to replace the previous word/phrase with:

Find and Replace	? ×
Fin**d** Re**p**lace **G**o To	
Fi**n**d what: Contract	⌄
Replace w**i**th: Agreement	⌄

5. If you would like to:
   a. See all the places where the word/phrase appears, then click "*Find Next*".
   b. Only replace the highlighted word/phrase in a specific place, click "*Replace*".

c. Replace the word/phrase in the entire document, click "*Replace All*":

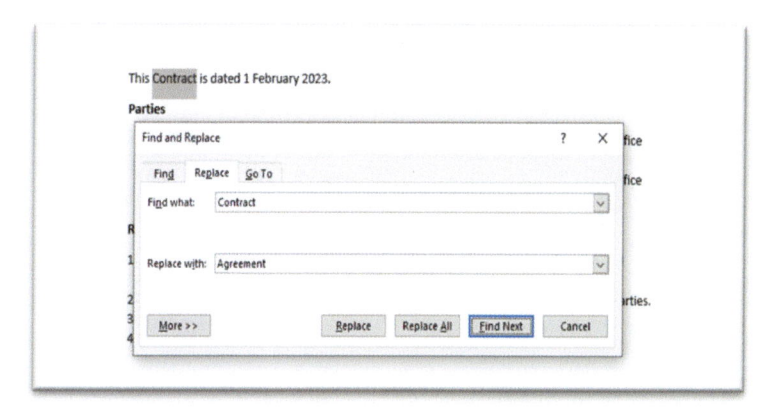

4. Finding Key Words and Phrases

Benefits

- Less time consuming, as the search results are instant; and
- Allows you to focus on reviewing and extracting relevant parts of the document.

Example

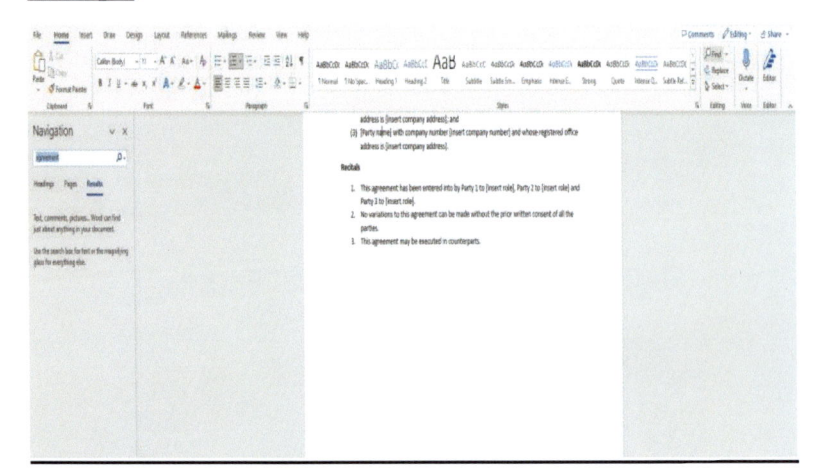

How to use

1. Press and hold down "*ctrl*" and "*f*", then type in the key words/phrases you are searching for:

OR

13

2. Click on the "*Home*" tab and click on "*Find*", then type in the key words/phrases you are searching for:

3. Search results are instant and you can navigate your way through the document using the up arrow for the previous search result and down arrow for the next search result:

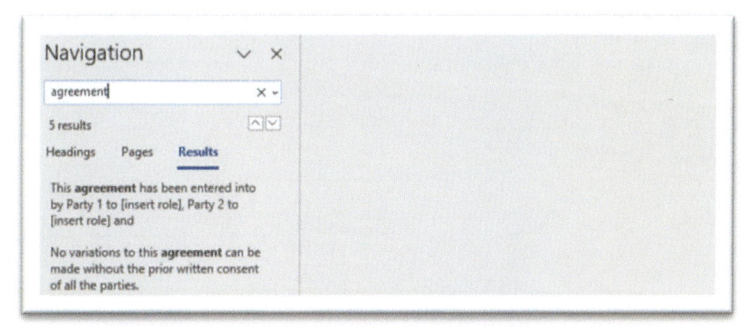

4. After you have finished searching, then you can click the "*x*" in the search box:

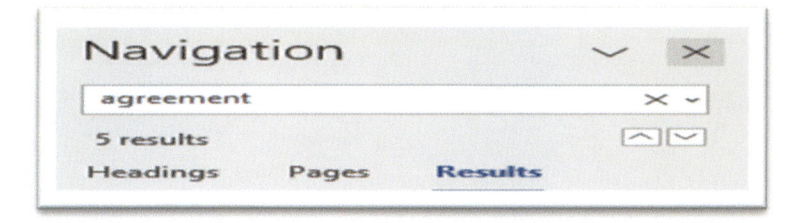

5. Changing "Cases" Without Re-Typing The Whole Paragraph

Benefits

- Avoids typing errors and mistakes; and
- Improved efficiency and time management.

Example

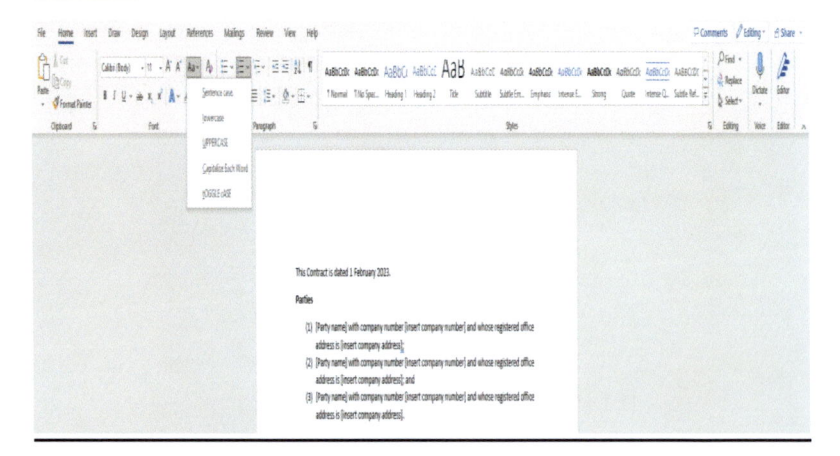

How to use

1. Click on the "*Home*" tab and click on "*Aa*", which is change case:

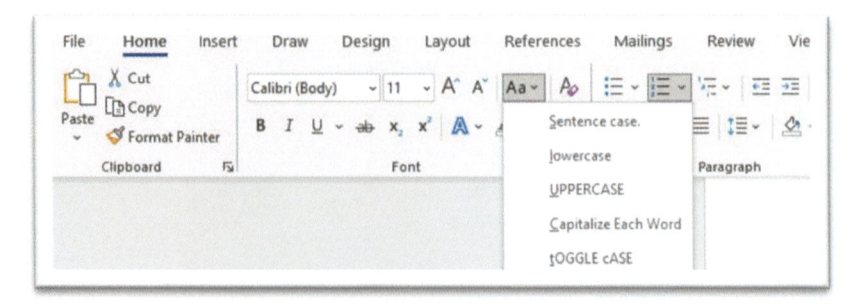

2. To:
    a. Capitalise the first letter of the sentence only, click "*Sentence case*".
    b. Remove all capital letters, click "*lowercase*".
    c. Capitalise every letter in the sentence, click "*UPPERCASE*".
    d. Capitalise the first letter of each word, click "*Capitalize Each Word*".
    e. Use both capital letters and lowercase, click "*tOGGLE cASE*".

6. Delete Extra Pages

Benefits

- Prevents the use of unnecessary space; and
- Improves document formatting.

Example

How to use

1. Click at the top of that page and press the *"backspace"* key:

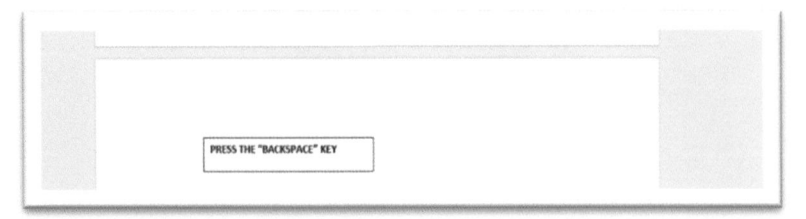

OR

2. Click on the "*View*" tab:
   a. Then "*Navigation*":

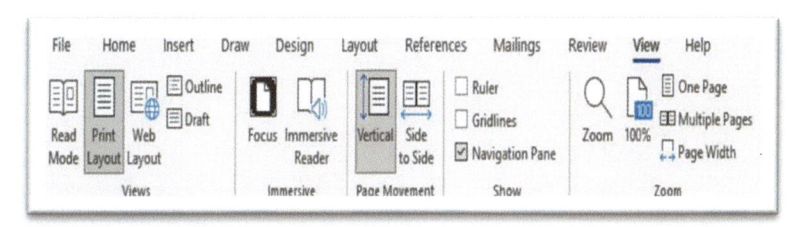

   b. Click on Pages:

   c. In the left panel, select the blank page thumbnail and press the "*backspace*" key:

7. Insert Page Numbers

Benefits

- Makes it easier to refer to relevant sections of the document; and
- Improves document formatting and presentation.

Example

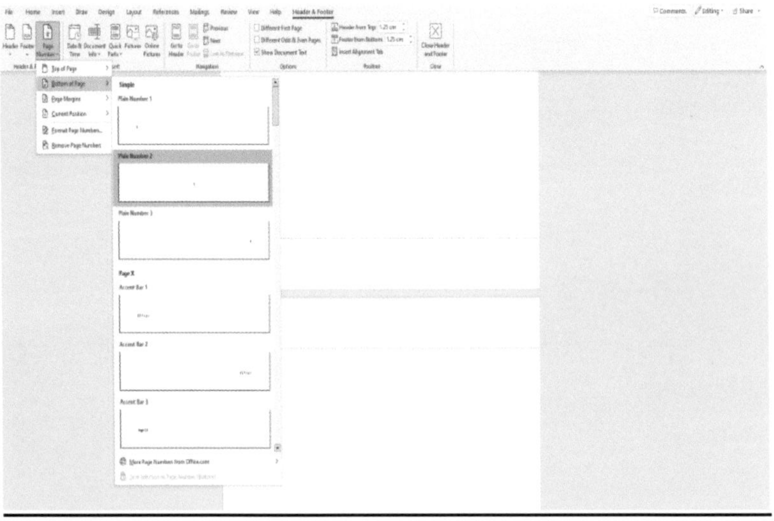

How to use

1. Click on the "*Insert*" tab.
2. Click on page numbers and then choose the location and style, for example:
   a. If you want page numbers at the top, click "*header*" and the thumbnail showing a page number on either the left, middle or right side of the document:

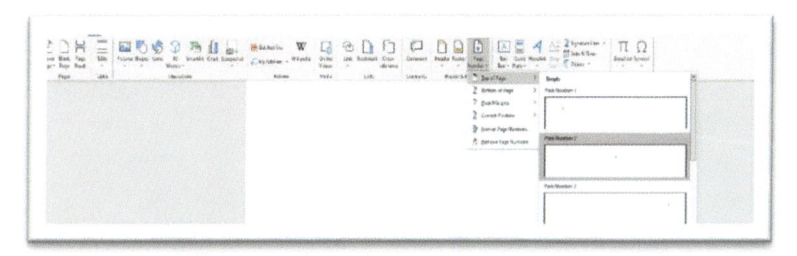

b. If you want page numbers at the bottom, click *"footer"* and the thumbnail showing a page number on either the left, middle or right side of the document:

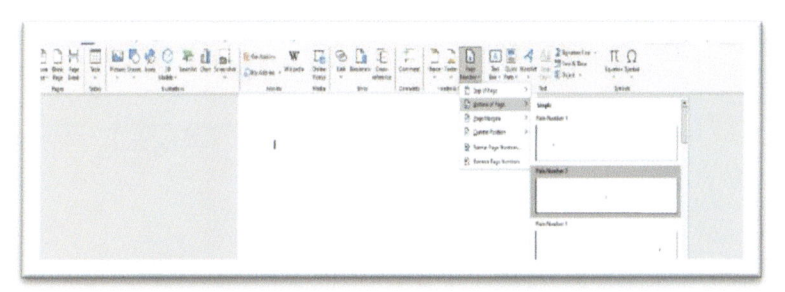

c. If you do not want a page number on the first page, click on the footer on the first page and select *"Different First Page"*:

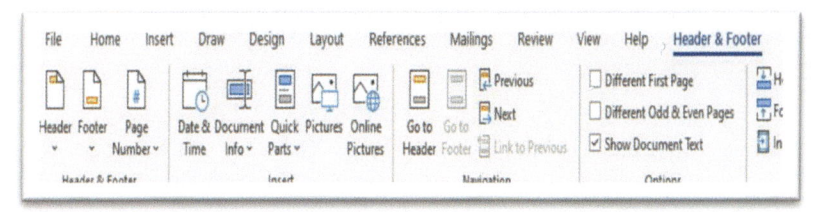

d. If you want the numbering to start at a specific number on a specific page, click on "*Page Number*", then "*Format Page Numbers*" and insert a number in "*Start at*":

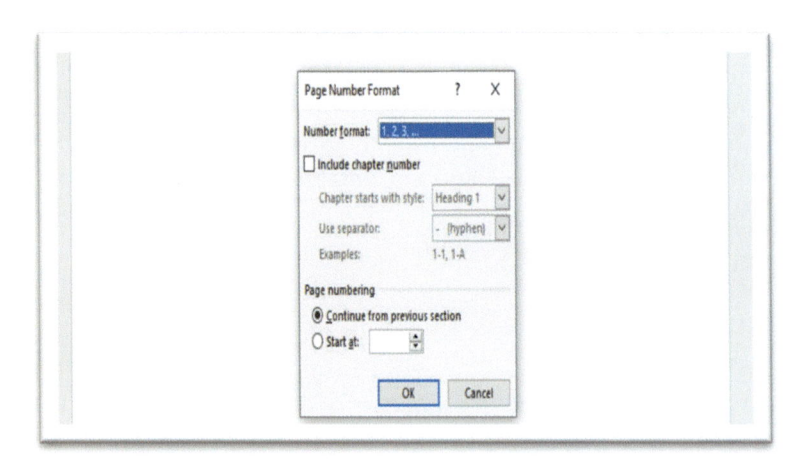

8. Add Execution/Signature Pages

Benefits

- It is easier and clearer for the respective parties to sign the documents; and
- Improves the layout of the document.

Example

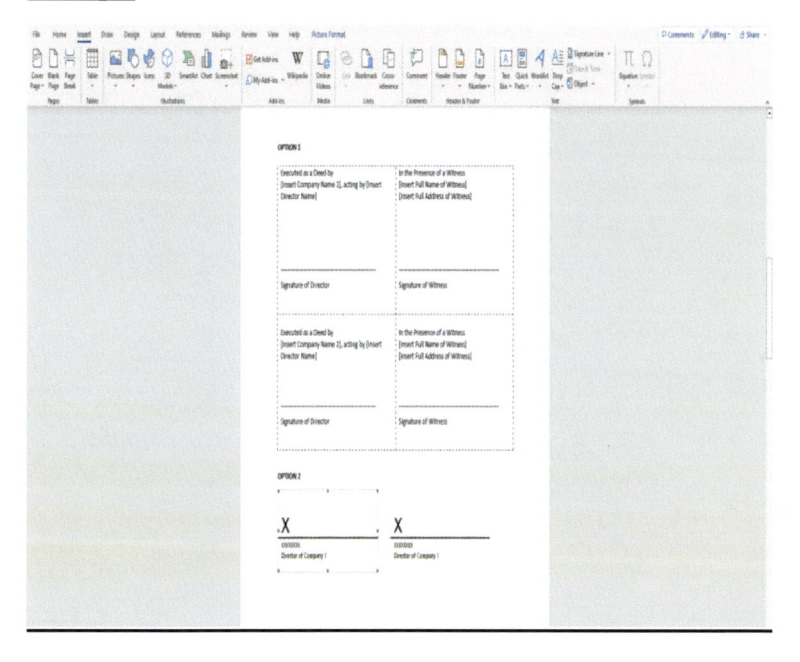

How to use

1. Click on the "*Insert*" tab:
   a. Click on table and subject to the number of parties who need to sign/execute the document, click 2x2:

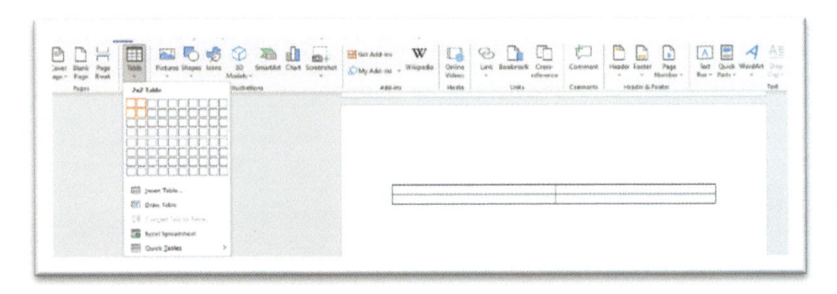

   b. In the left column, insert either "*Signed by*" or "*Executed as a Deed by*", then the company/individual's details:

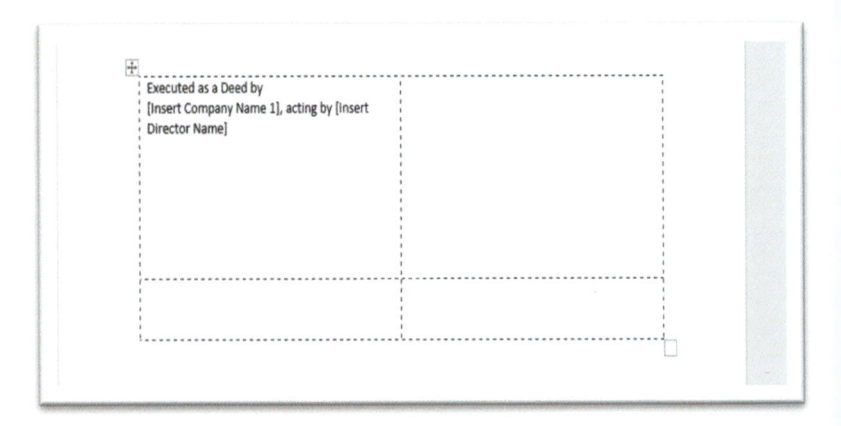

c. Underneath that, click the *"Underline"* sign and hold down the space bar until a signature line appears. Below that, insert *"Signature of Director or Individual"*:

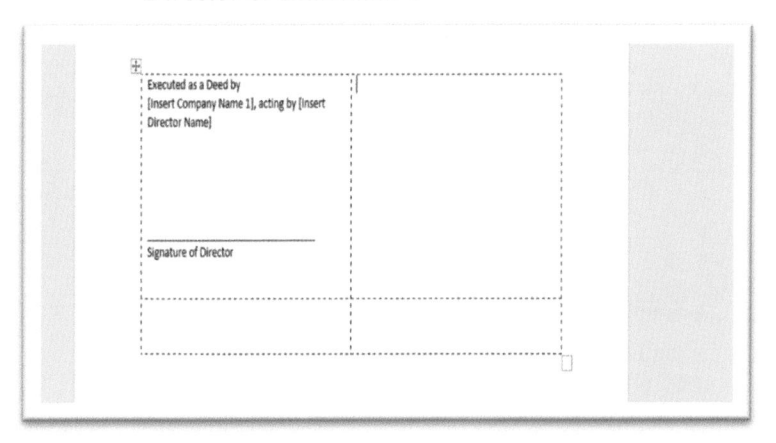

d. Copy and paste this into the right column and the rows below, changing any details where necessary:

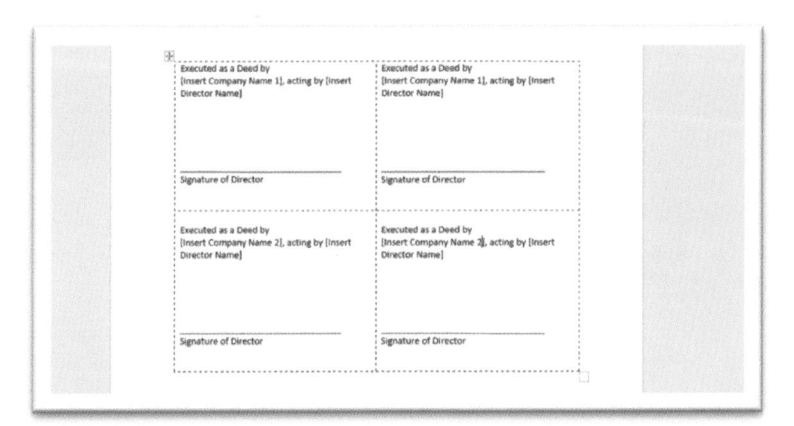

e. If a witness will be required to sign the document, in the right column, insert "*In the presence of*", insert the witness details, then add a signature line as above and insert "*Signature of Witness*":

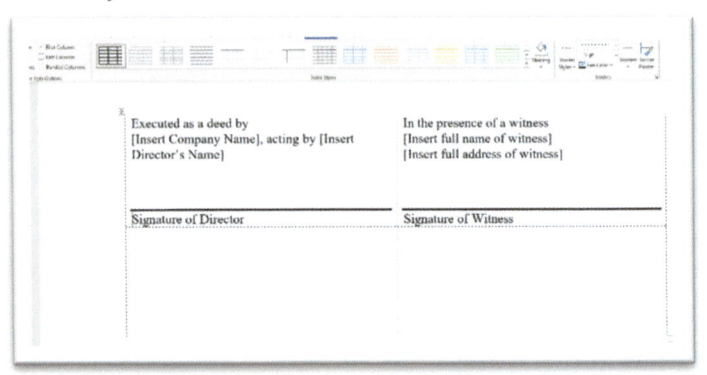

OR

2. Click where you want a signature line:
   a. Click the "*Insert*" tab, then "*Signature Line*":

b. Click "*Microsoft Signature Line*":

c. In the setup box, insert the name in the "*Suggested signer*" box and insert the title/role in the "*Suggested signer's title*":

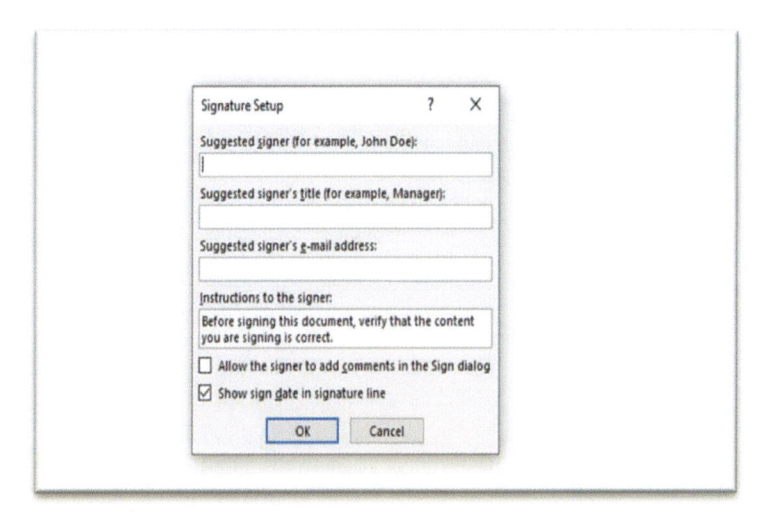

9. Comparing Documents

Benefits

- Less time consuming;
- Excellent attention to detail; and
- Efficient analysis of any amendments made to documents, especially those which have been previously agreed between parties and need to be signed.

Example

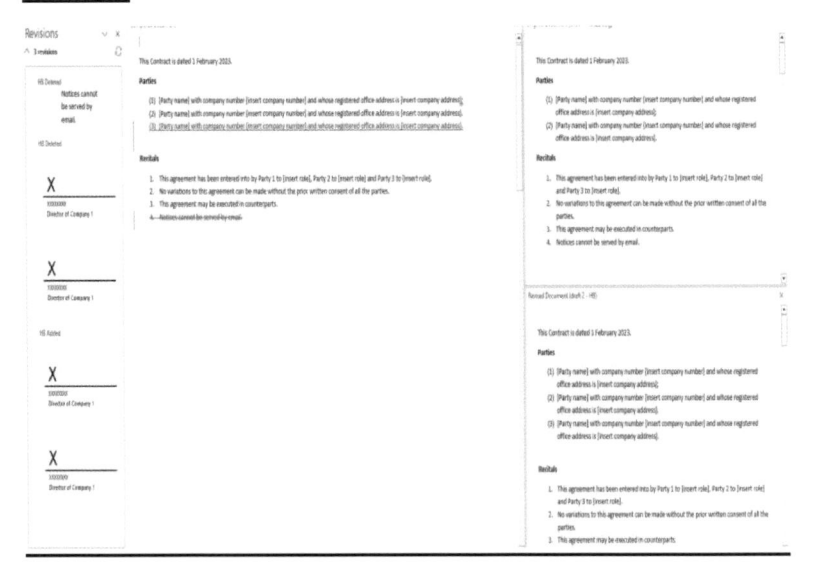

How to use

1. Click on the "*Review*" tab.
2. Then click on "*Compare*" twice:

3. Click on the image of the folder on the left side of the box, to select the original document and double-click on this document.
4. Then click on the image of the folder on the right side of the box, to select the revised document and double-click on this document:

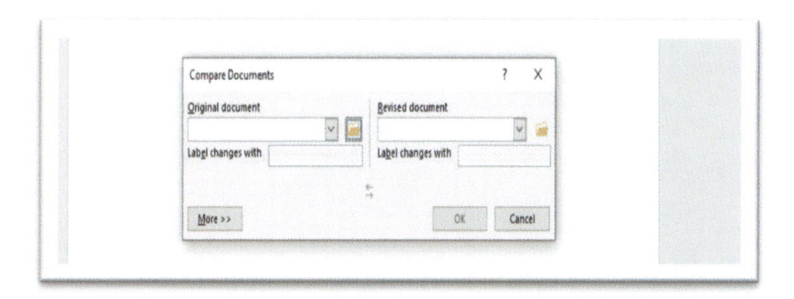

5. In the "*label unmarked changes with*" box, you can insert the name you want to appear to identify any changes to the documents:

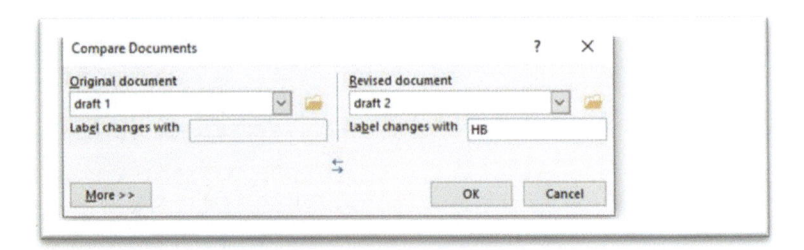

6. You can click on "*more*" to amend the comparison settings and choose what changes you want identified, by clicking/checking the boxes and those you do not want identified, by unclicking/unchecking the boxes:

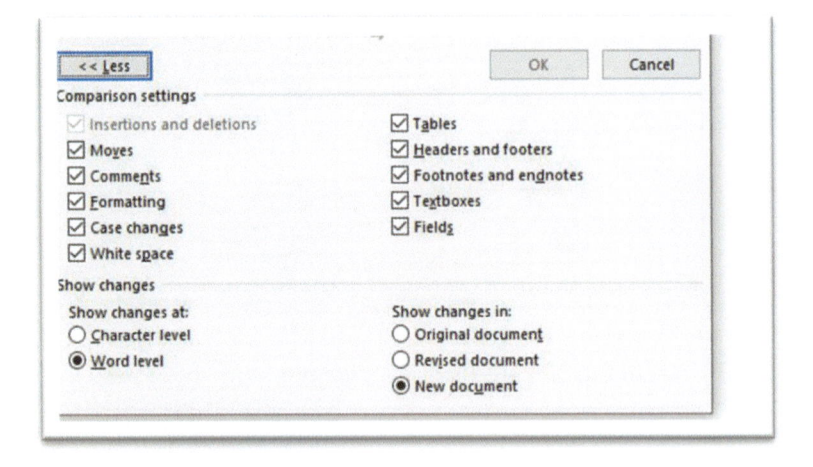

7. Then click "*OK*"
8. The screen will be divided into three sections. Any changes will appear on the left side and also in a different colour in the middle/main screen e.g. strikeouts for words that have been deleted and

underline for words that have been inserted. The original and revised documents will appear on the right side (one above the other):

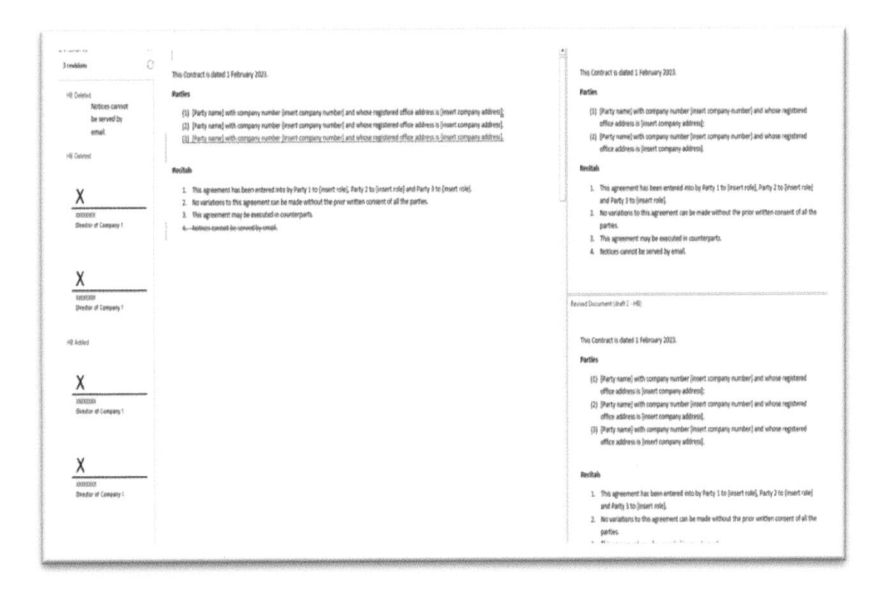

10. Combining Documents

Benefits

- Less time consuming; and
- Enables multiple parties to work on various versions of the document and simplifies the process of combining the document.

Example

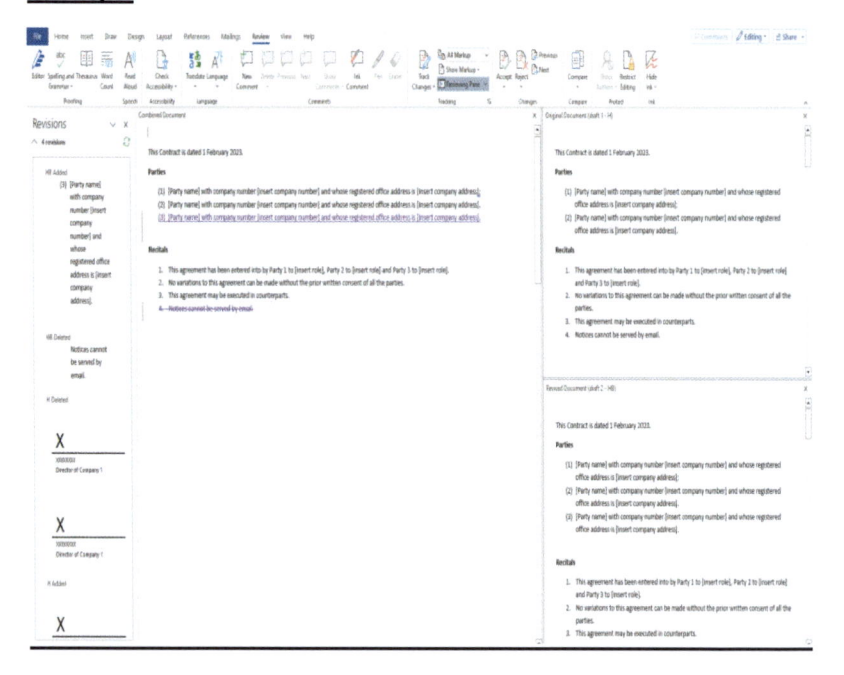

How to use

1. Click on the "*Review*" tab.
2. Then click on "*Compare*", then "*Combine*":

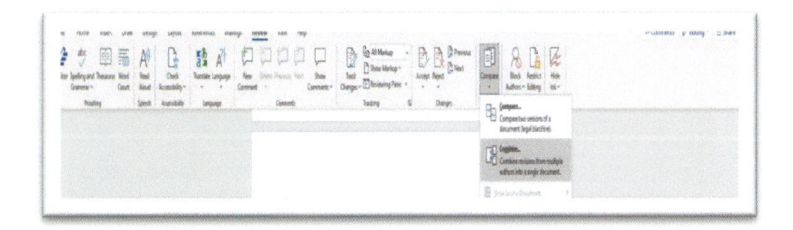

3. Click on the image of the folder on the left side of the box, to select the original document and double-click on this document.

4. Then click on the image of the folder on the right side of the box, to select the revised document and double-click on this document:

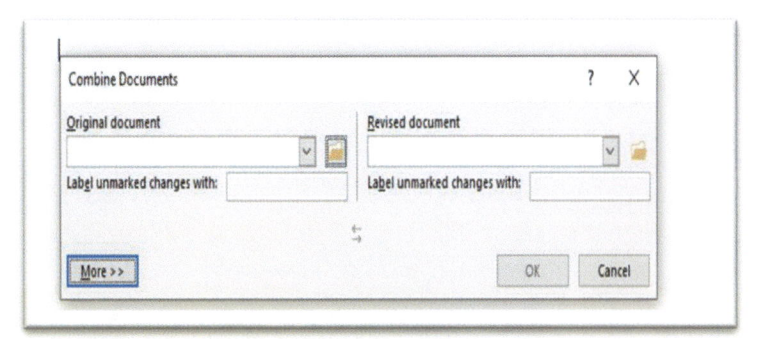

5. In the "*label unmarked changes with*" box, you can insert the name you want to appear to identify any changes to the documents:

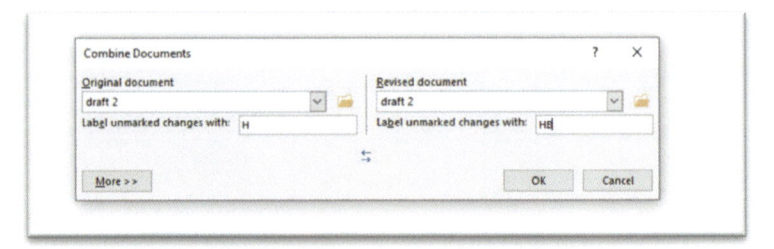

6. You can click on "*more*" to amend the combined settings and choose what changes you want identified, by clicking/checking the boxes and those you do not want identified, by unclicking/unchecking the boxes:

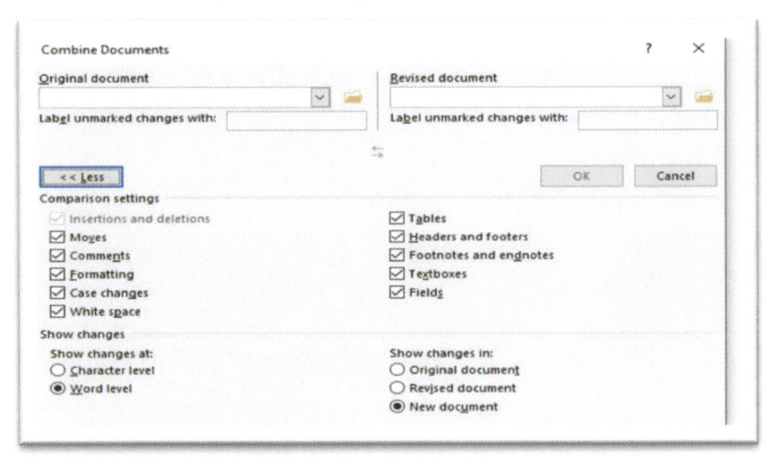

7. Then click "*OK*".
8. The screen will be divided into three sections. Any changes will appear on the left side and also in a different colour in the middle/main screen e.g. strikeouts for words that have been deleted and underline for words that have been inserted. The original and revised documents will appear on the right side (one above the other):

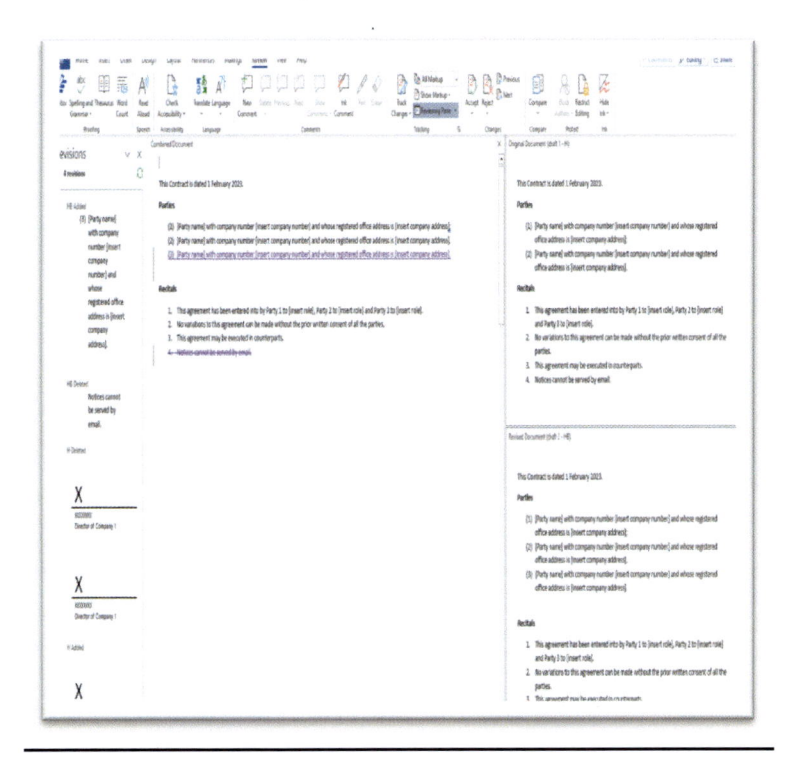

11. Using Watermarks

Benefits

- Shows the status of the document e.g. draft documents or confidential documents; and
- Prevents unauthorised use of the document.

Example

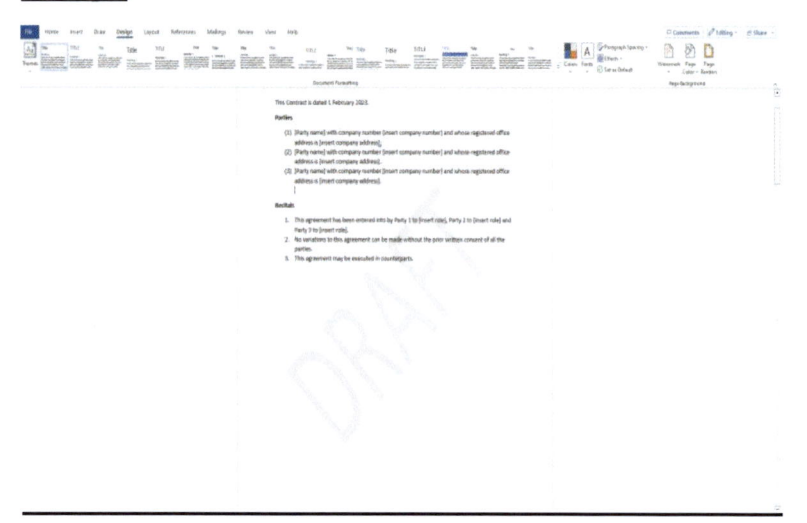

How to use

1. Click on the "*Design*" tab.
2. Click on "*Watermark*":

3. Then select and click the type of watermark you intend on using (confidential or disclaimers such as draft). The watermark is then added to the document:

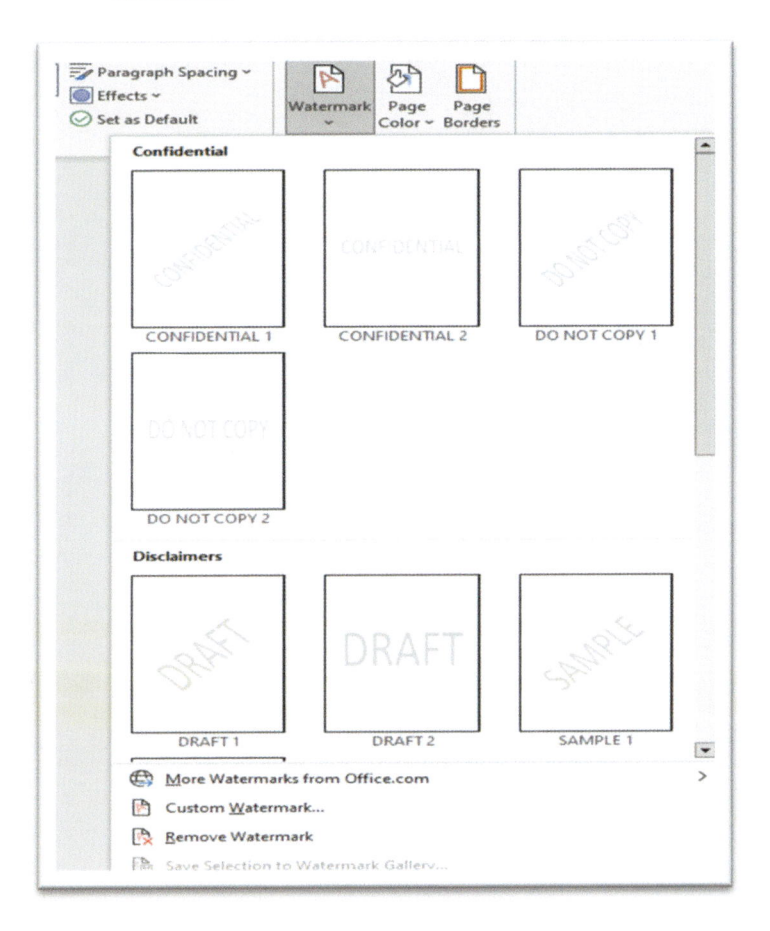

4. You can also create a bespoke watermark by clicking on "Custom Watermark", then either selecting:
   a. *"Picture Watermark"*, if you intend on inserting the company logo or a different image; or
   b. *"Text Watermark"*, if you would like to replace the text:

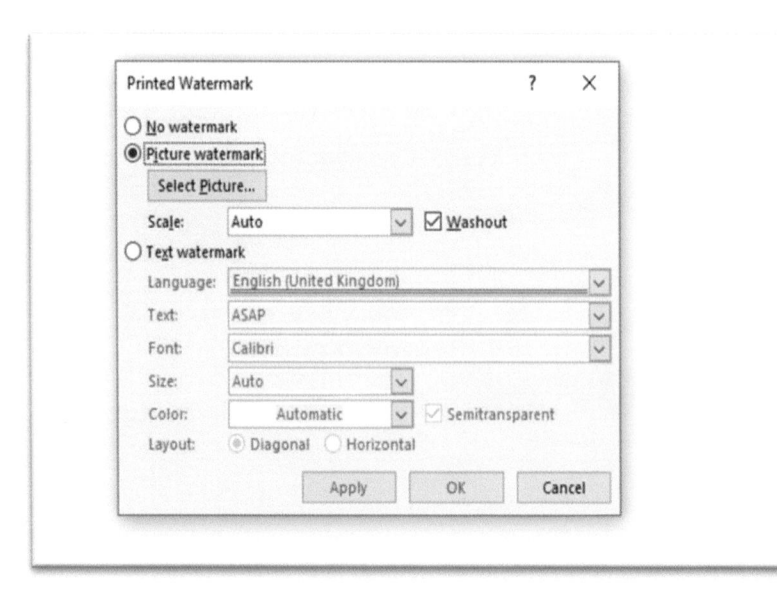

12. Inserting Rows In Tables Faster

Benefits

- Increases efficiency; and
- Automatically splits the table into the relevant number of columns.

Example

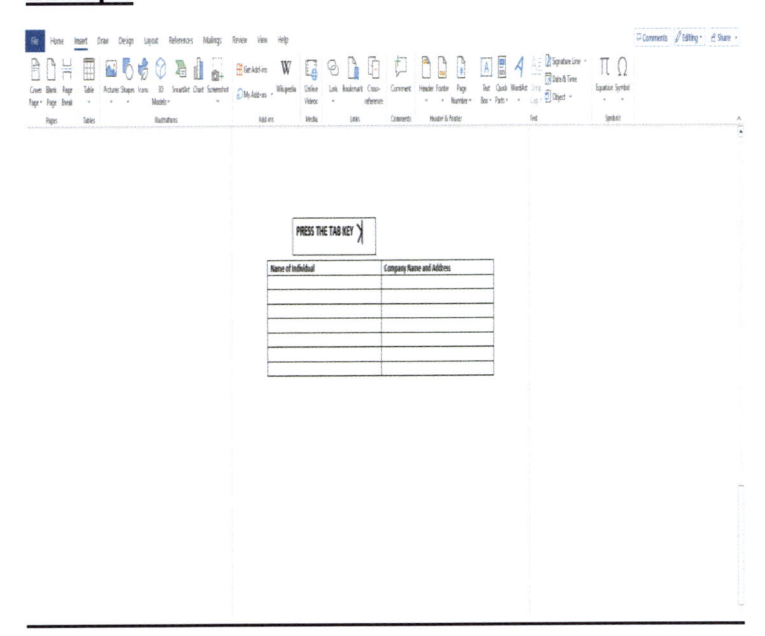

How to use

1. Click on the "*Insert*" tab.

2. Click on "*Table*" and select one row and the number of columns required e.g. 2x3 or 4x1:

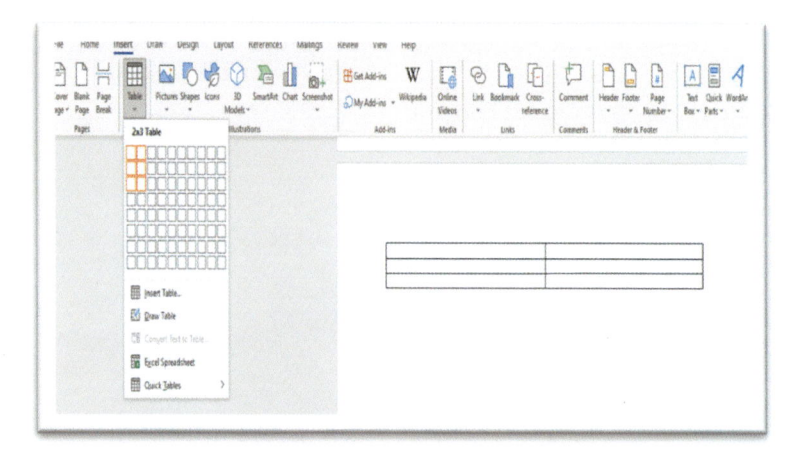

3. Then click on the row and keep pressing the "*Tab*" key, until you reach the desired number of rows you require.

13. Copy and Paste Text Without Re-Formatting

Benefits

- Increases efficiency; and
- Automatically merges the style of the copied text into the document text.

Example

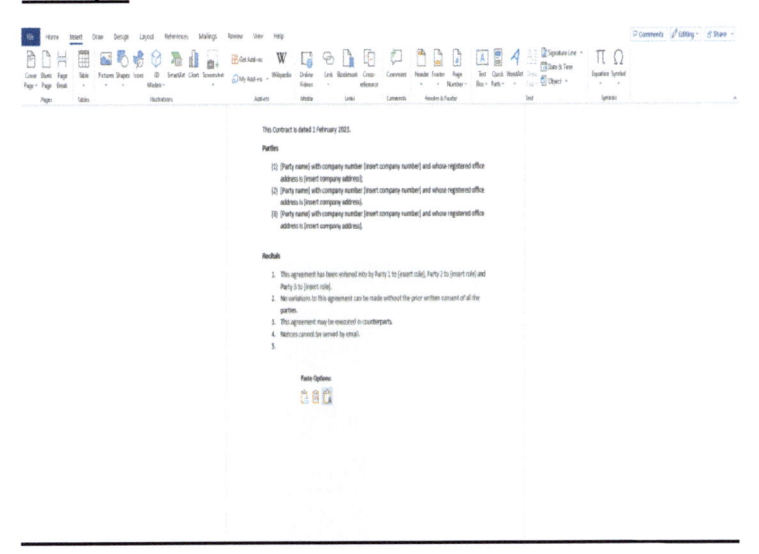

How to use

1. Copy the text from the relevant document:

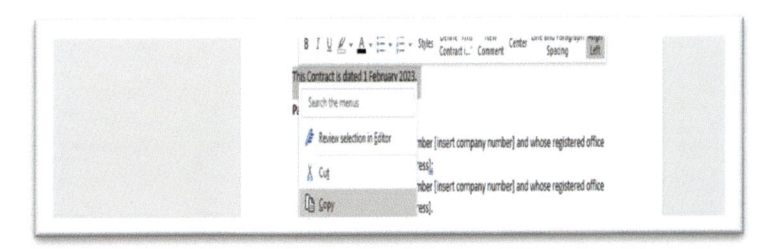

2. Right click on the section of the document where you want to insert the text:

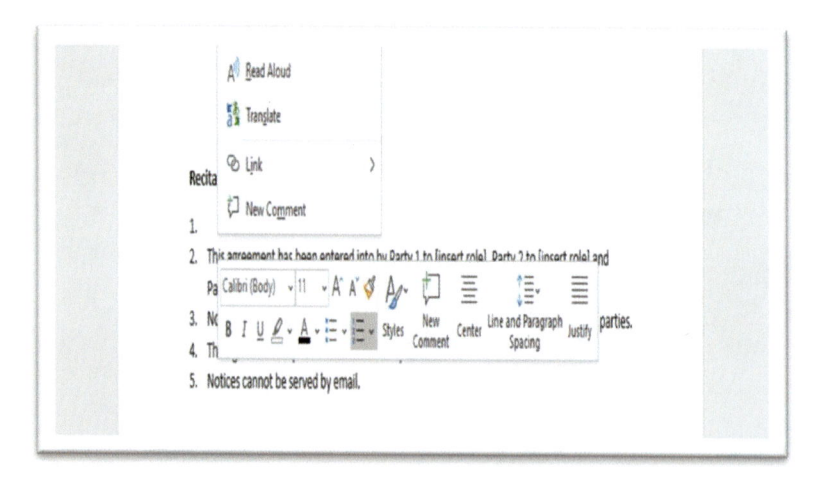

3. From the paste options, click on "*Keep Text Only*". This will paste the copied text to match the rest of the font and style used in the document you are editing:

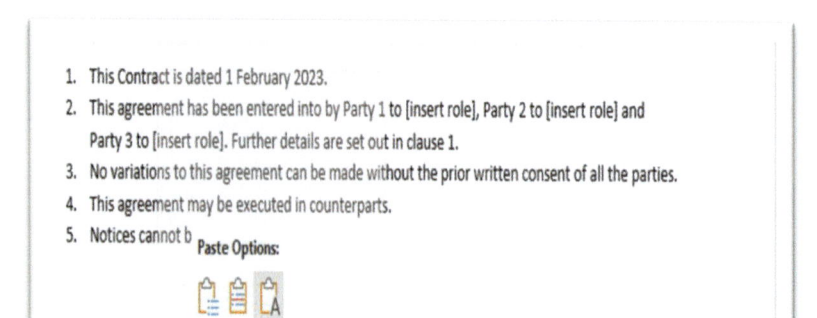

4. If you want to:
   a. Paste text exactly how it appears from the copied source, click "*Keep Source Formatting*" or press and hold "*Ctrl*" and "*V*"; or
   b. Convert the copied text into an image, click "*Picture*":

> **Recitals**
>
> Recitals
>
> 1. This Contract is dated 1 February 2023.
> 2. This agreement has been entered into by Party 1 to [insert role], Party 2 to [insert role] and Party 3 to [insert role]. Further details are set out in clause 1.
> 3. No variations to this agreement can be made without the prior written consent of all the parties.
> 4. This agreement may be executed in counterparts.
> 5. Notices ca
>
> Paste Options:
>
> 1.

14. Formatting Contents Page

Benefits

- Increases efficiency; and
- Minimises the risk of errors in relation to incorrect headings and page numbers.

Example

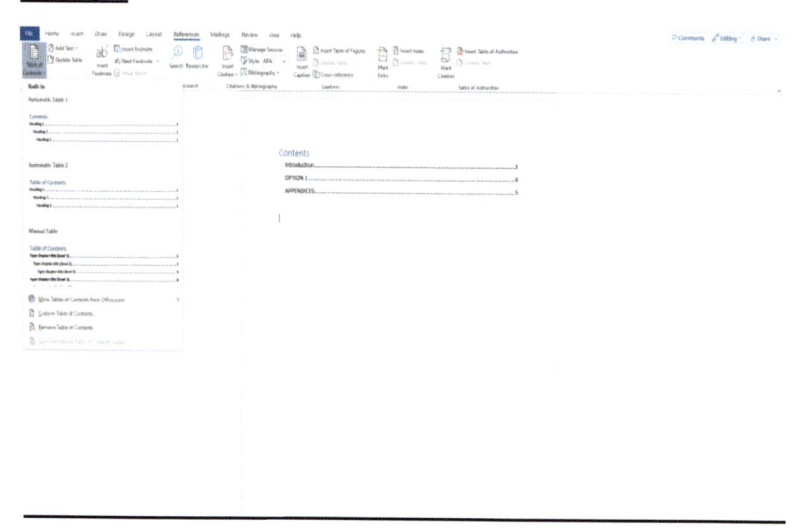

How to use

1. Whilst drafting the document, ensure any headings are added using one of the "*Headings*" styles under the "*Home*" tab:

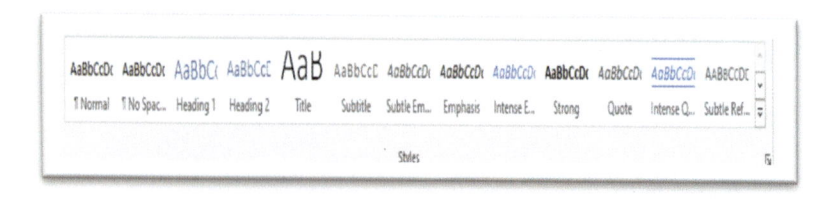

2. Once you have finished drafting your document, click on the page where you intend on inserting the contents page.

3. Click on the "*References*" tab and "*Insert Table of Contents*", then choose your preferred style:

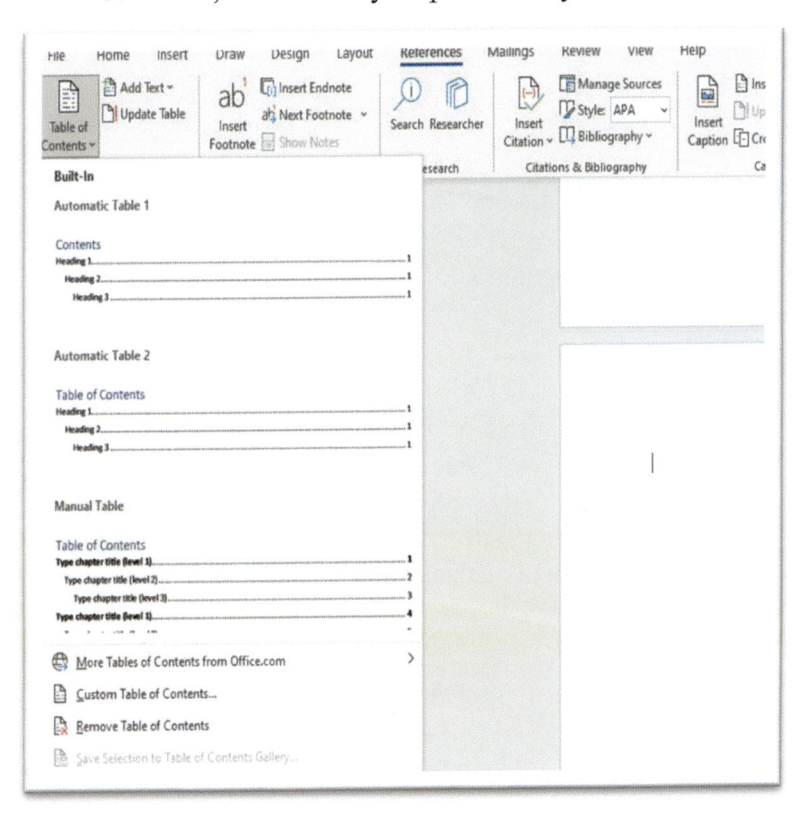

4. If you make any amendments to the headings or the page numbers have changed, go the contents page, right click the table and select "*Update Field*":

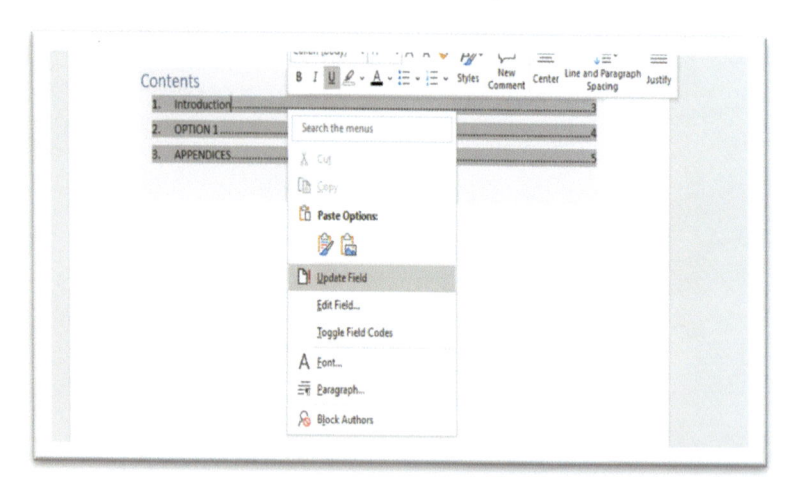

5. You then have the option to "*Update page numbers only*" or "*Update entire table*". The second option is preferable when you have updated the title of the headings, in addition to where the location of those headings/sections has changed:

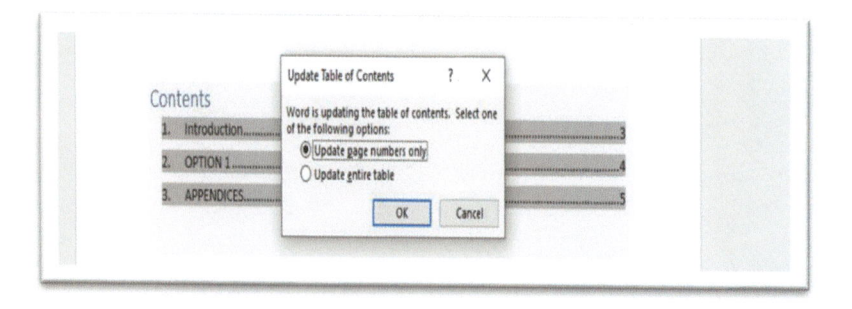

15. Inserting Clause Numbers

Benefits

- More efficient and automatically continues numbering, without manual input; and
- Reduces formatting errors.

Example

> 1. Clause 1
>   1.1. Sub-Clause 1.1
>   1.2. Sub-Clause 1.2
>   1.3. Sub-Clause 1.3
> 2. Clause 2
>   2.1. Sub-Clause 2.1

How to use

1. Click on the "*Home*" tab.
2. Under the "*Paragraph*" section, click "*Multi-level list*":

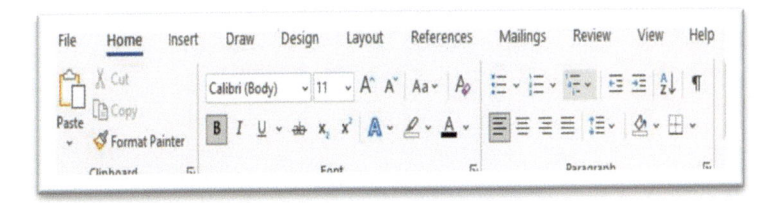

3. Click the numbering style you intend on using and start drafting:

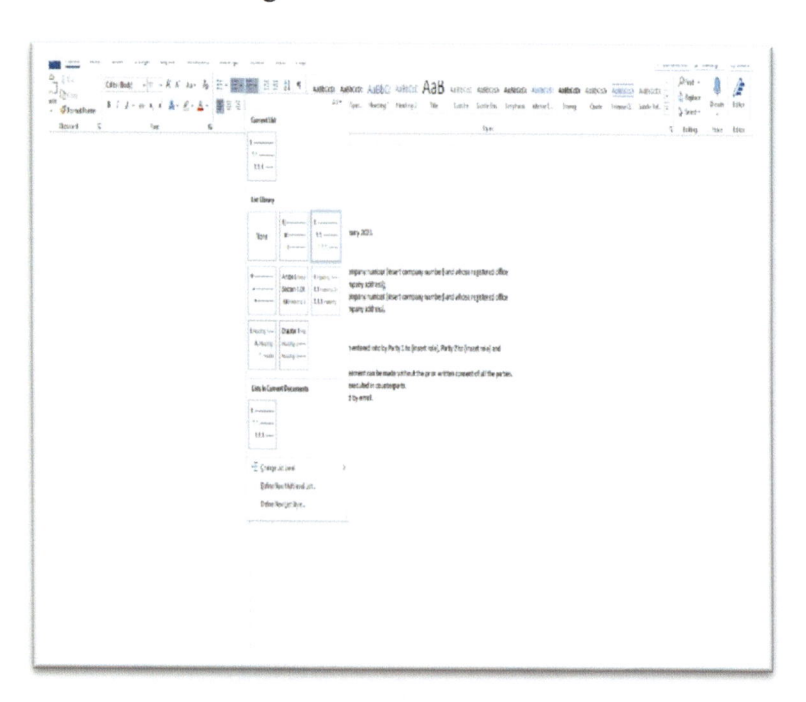

16. Cross Reference and Hyperlink Clause Numbers

Benefits

- More efficient and changes the reference to clause numbers, without manual input;
- Reduces the risk of incorrect reference to clauses.

Example

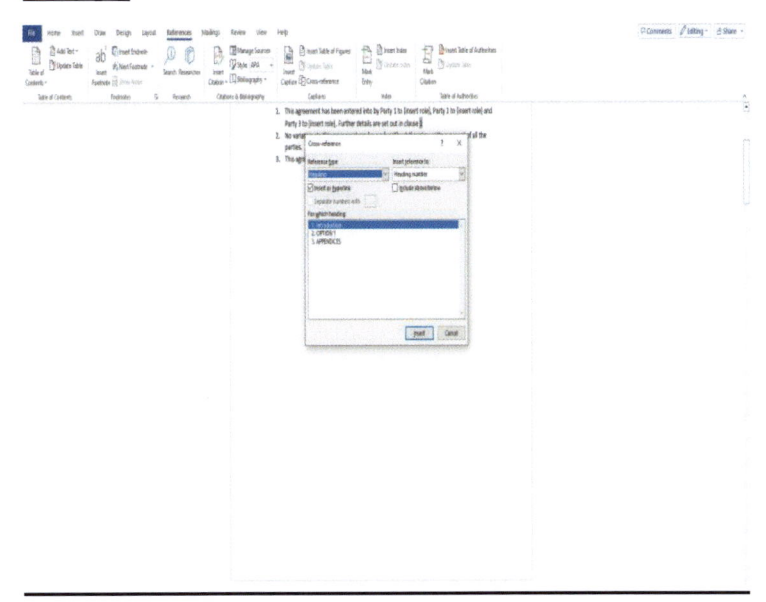

How to use

1. Click on the "*Insert*" tab and "*Cross-reference*":

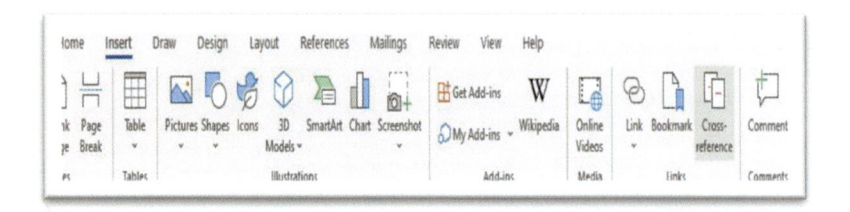

2. From the "*Reference type*" box, select the item you want to link the clause to, for example, the heading:

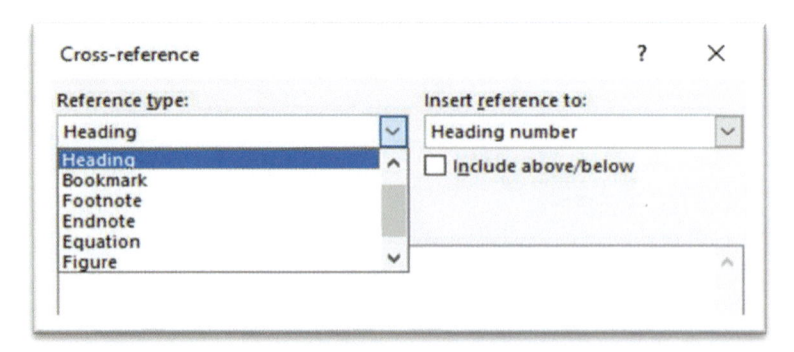

3. In the "*Insert reference to*" box, select the item you want inserted in the document e.g. Heading number:

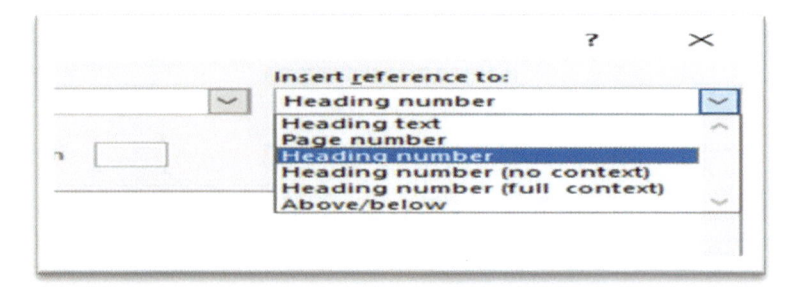

4. In the *"For which"* box, click the specific item you want to refer to e.g. insert the cross-reference:

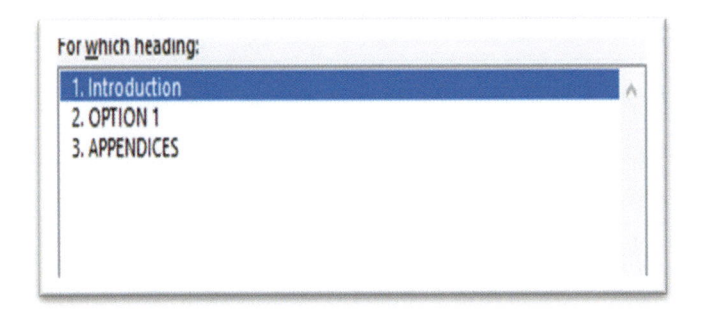

```
For which heading:
1. Introduction
2. OPTION 1
3. APPENDICES
```

5. Click Insert.
6. If you intend on allowing individuals to be directed straight to the relevant clause number, tick the *"Insert as hyperlink"* box before proceeding to step 5 and clicking *"Insert"*:

```
☑ Insert as hyperlink       ☐ Include above/below
☐ Separate numbers with [   ]
For which heading:
```

7. Highlight all the document and click on one of the clause numbers, then select *"Update Field"* to ensure the clause numbers are correct and reflect any changes made:

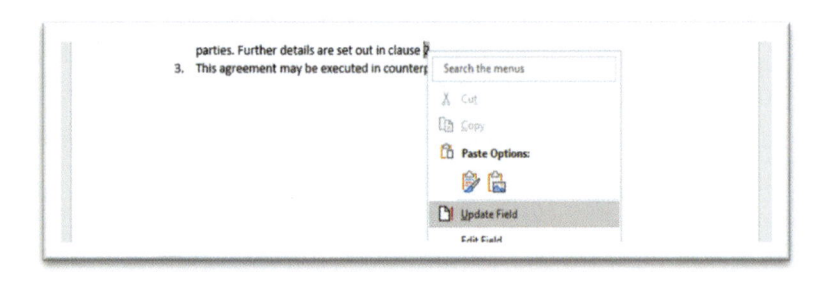

parties. Further details are set out in clause
3. This agreement may be executed in counterp...

Search the menus
✂ Cut
📋 Copy
Paste Options:
📋 📋
📄 Update Field
Edit Field

17. Protect The Document
Benefits

- Maintains confidentiality and prevents data breach; and
- Allows only specific individuals to access and amend the document.

Example

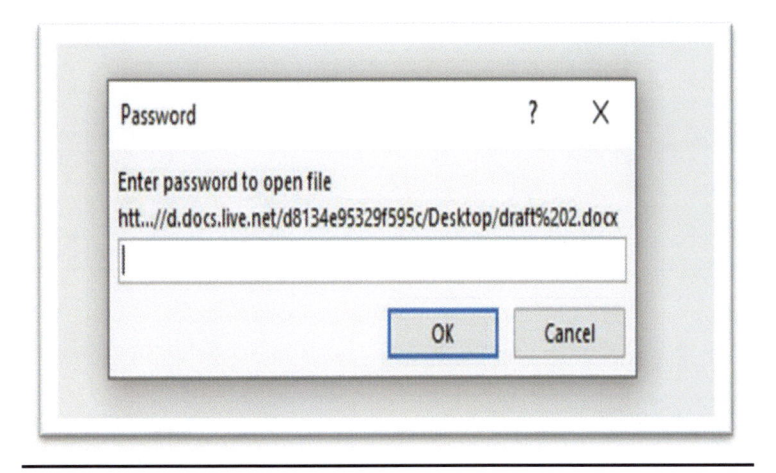

How to use

1. Click on the "*File*" tab.
2. Click on "*Info*", then "*Protect Document*" and "*Encrypt with Password*":

3. Keep the password safe and save the file to ensure the document can only be accessed with a password.

18. Convert The Document To A PDF (Portable Document Format)

Benefits

- Secure and prevents the document from being amended, once it has been finalised;
- Can be accessed on various devices; and
- Easy to use.

Example

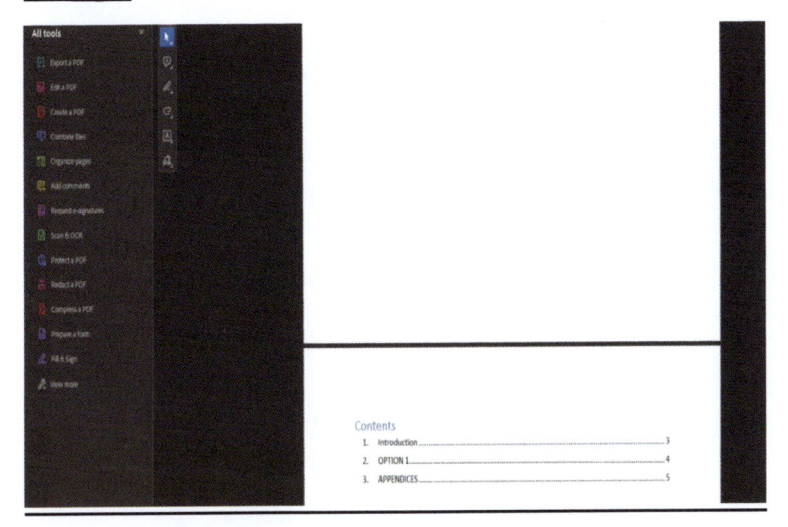

How to use

1. Click on the "*File*" tab and "*Save as*".
2. Rename the document and click on "Browse" to choose where you intend on saving the file:

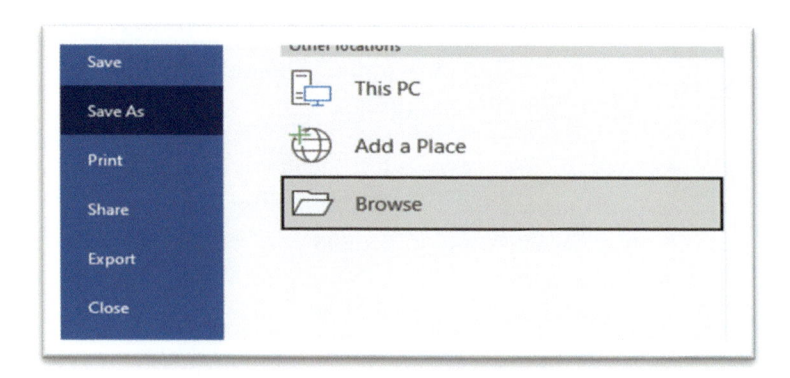

3. Change the "*Save as type*" from word to "*PDF*":

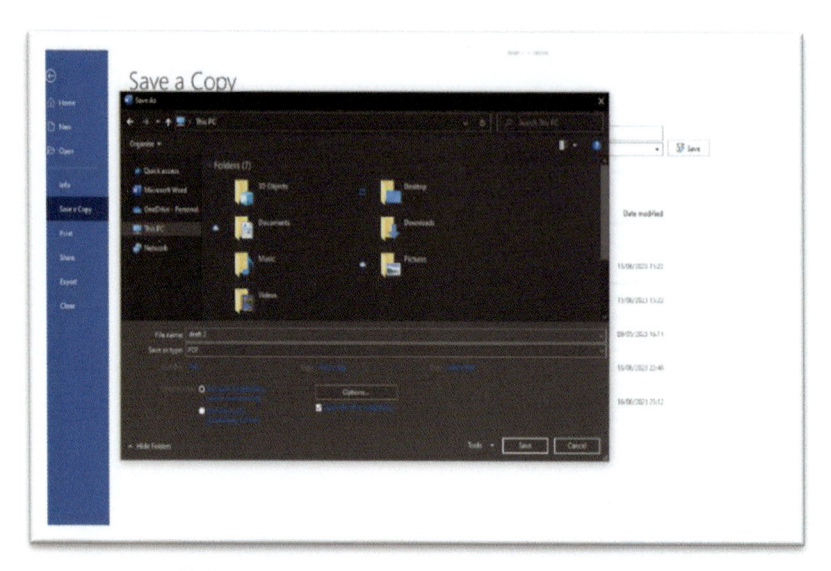

4. Click "*Save*" and the PDF has been created.

Printed in Great Britain
by Amazon